CW00926260

Cicely Mary Barker and her Art

Cicely Mary Barker and her Art

Jane Laing

Frederick Warne

FREDERICK WARNE

Published by the Penguin Group
27 Wrights Lane, London W8 5TZ, England
Penguin Books USA Inc., 375 Hudson Street, New York, New York 10014, USA
Penguin Books Australia Ltd, Ringwood, Victoria, Australia
Penguin Books Canada Ltd, 2801 John Street, Markham, Ontario, Canada L3R 1B4
Penguin Books (NZ) Ltd, 182-190 Wairau Road, Auckland 10, New Zealand

Penguin Books Ltd, Registered Offices: Harmondsworth, Middlesex, England

First published 1995
3 5 7 9 10 8 6 4

ISBN 0 7232 4051 5

Designed by Design 23

Colour origination by Saxon
Printed in China

British Library Cataloguing In Publication Data available

Contents

Introduction

Cicely Mary Barker was born at home at 68 Waddon Road, West Croydon in Surrey, on 28 June 1895, two years before Queen Victoria's Diamond Jubilee, and three years before the death of one of her favourite artists – Edward Burne-Jones. She was the second daughter of Mary (née Oswald – from an old Croydon family) and Walter Barker. She suffered from epilepsy as a child, and all her life was somewhat delicate physically. Her parents nurtured their frail daughter through childhood, protecting her as much as possible

Cicely Mary Barker's parents, Mary and Walter.

Above: Dorothy and Cicely as babies.
Right: Cicely with her nurse.
The photograph is labelled, 'First day downstairs after 3 months illness'.

from the world outside. Later, her sister Dorothy (her elder by two years) continued to do this. The family was moderately well off, falling into the lower end of the upper middle class of English society. Her father was – like his father before him – a partner in a seed supply company. They could afford to live in a sizeable Victorian house in a middle-class suburb, to employ a nanny for Cicely, a cook and a maid. The cook, Rose Bucknell (known affectionately as 'Rose Bose'), was taken on in 1897 and part of her remit was to cook 'special meals' for Cicely. They also employed a governess for Cicely in order that she could be educated at home.

Confined, for the most part, to the house, and often to her bed, Cicely spent much of her childhood without the company of other children, and depended on herself for amusement. She showed an early talent for drawing and her parents fostered her interest. As a young child she was given Kate Greenaway's *Under the Window* (1878) and many Kate Greenaway painting books, in which the outline illustrations were provided alongside coloured examples. Where Cicely has completed these illustrations, her work is meticulous. She was also given several of Randolph Caldecott's picture books: *The Fox Jumps Over the Parson's Gate*, *The*

Some of Cicely's childhood books.

Three watercolour paintings
by Walter Barker.

Above: a painting by Cicely at the age of eleven.
Right: a watercolour by Walter.

Farmer's Boy, *Hey Diddle Diddle* and *Baby Bunting*. Later, she incorporated elements of both these artists' work in her own illustrations.

Her father, in particular, encouraged her talents, for he too was an accomplished artist. In 1908, when Cicely was thirteen, he enrolled her at Croydon Art Society, where they both exhibited work. He also paid for a correspondence course in art, which provided her with much detailed and constructive criticism, and which she continued until at least 1919. It was her father who, in 1911, took examples of Cicely's work to the popular printer Raphael Tuck. The company replied on 3 October 1911:

> With reference to your visit this morning, I can take four of the little drawings your daughter left with me, if she would care to accept half a sovereign for the four. Of course, on the understanding that they are absolutely original?

On sending the cheque two days later, the company representative commented: 'I shall always be pleased to see anything that your daughter may care to submit.'

In October 1911, Cicely won second prize in a poster competition run by Croydon Art Society. An art critic for the *Croydon Advertiser* commented: 'Her entry was a noteworthy example of poster design. Her drawings

The Barker family on holiday in Swanage in 1907.

show a remarkable freedom of spirit. She has distinct promise.' The same year she was elected a life member of Croydon Art Society – at 16 years old, she was the youngest to receive this honour.

Although clouded by illness, Cicely's childhood seems to have been a secure and happy one. The family moved twice – to 'Heathside', 1 Duppas Avenue in 1899, and to 17 The Waldrons in 1907 – but they stayed within the Croydon area. They went on holidays together, usually to the seaside, where Cicely sketched alongside her father; and they extended their home to Mary's mother, Eleanor Oswald, in 1907 when her husband, Charles Oswald, died. Eleanor herself died in December 1921, aged 91. In *Old Rhymes for All Times* (1928), Cicely remembered her grandmother with much affection in the Preface, beginning:

> When I was a little girl, I had a very dear Granny, who used to sing me some old nursery songs which I have never heard from anyone else, or seen anywhere in print. The chief of these were 'John and his Mare' and 'Tingle-tangle Titmouse'.

There was always a dog in the Barker household. Cicely sent many cards to her sister and mother throughout her life depicting one of the family's dogs, and as a child she painted a set of cards, called the 'Bow Wow family'. These were: Dot Barker, the Bow Wow's daughter; Mrs Barker, the Bow Wow's Wife; Mr Barker, the Bow Wow; and

Above: Dorothy Barker with the family dog, captioned, 'Nanny as a baby'.

Right: one of the 'Bow Wow' set of cards.

A portrait of Cicely in her teens.

(revealingly) Cis Barker, the Bow Wow's Baby.

Because of her gentle disposition and years of suffering, Cicely was treated affectionately as the baby of the family and over-protected all her life. A note from Walter Barker to his daughter on her fifteenth birthday indicates that he was a devoted father. It reads:

> Many happy returns of the day my best Ciskin, my present to you is a picture from Price's which you are to go with me to choose, as soon after breakfast as is convenient to you. Best love darling, from your father.

Cicely's first correspondence art tutor also wrote to her using the diminutive 'Ciskin', while her later tutor, Alice B Woodward, began a letter to her in 1918 with 'My dear child'. Cicely was actually 23 years old.

Walter Barker's death on 3 June 1912 at the age of 43 dealt a devastating blow to his immediate family and was also deeply felt by his business colleagues and friends at church. He died as a result of contracting a virus from a sample of corn he was testing. The *London Corn Circular* gave the following obituary:

> . . . it is sad to contemplate this brave spirit wrestling manfully with illness over a protracted period, and facing with resolute fortitude the many surgical operations that became necessary – fourteen in all – and then to think we are to lose him nevertheless. For many years a well-known and highly respected member of the seed market . . . this genial and ever-courteous gentleman.

The vicar of the parish church, St Edmund's, L J White-Thomson, wrote:

> The death of Mr Walter Barker after a long and most painful illness, borne with heroic courage, is not only a cause of wide-spread sorrow among his many personal friends, but also a sad loss to our Parish life. He will be greatly missed at St Edmund's, while his unselfish life has had an influence for good on all with whom he has been brought in contact. We thank God for his example.

The Barkers were a deeply religious family and they bore their terrible loss with Christian fortitude. The extended family supported them as much as they could – financially and emotionally – but it was Dorothy who took the responsibility for holding the immediate family together. While Cicely was educated at home, Dorothy had been sent to Woodford school to study. She went on to train there as a teacher in the kindergarten, bringing home a small salary. From there she went to another private school, Clayton's, but she disliked it. She wrote to her aunt Alice Oswald (who was the first woman to be appointed as a head Deaconess in the Church of England) at her ministry in Penarth, South Wales:

Deaconess Alice Oswald, Cicely's aunt.

Cicely used child models for this birthday greetings card.

> School breaks up on Saturday, for which I am more than glad, I have had quite enough of old Clayton, she seems to increase almost daily in her fussiness and un-business-likeness.

She looked for a post as a governess, and then decided to set up her own kindergarten. With this arrangement she could earn money for the family and keep a watchful eye over the household. In an interview with the *Croydon Advertiser* in October 1958, Cicely remembers:

> My sister ran a kindergarten and I used to borrow her students for models. For many years I had an atmosphere of children about me – I never forgot it.

Cicely also tried to alleviate the family's difficult financial position. She loved writing poetry as well as painting, and she began to sell examples of both to magazines such as *My Magazine* (edited by Arthur Nee), *Child's Own* magazine, and the *Leading Strings* and *Raphael Tuck* annuals. She exhibited paintings and sketches at Croydon Art Society and Women Artists' Exhibitions, and in 1918 the Royal Institute accepted 'A

A watercolour by Cicely of her sister Dorothy.

Fairy Song' for exhibition in the North Gallery. The sale price was £6.6.0.

She also entered art competitions, and in August 1914 she won a competition run by *The Challenge* for 'a portrait of the editor as I imagine him to be'. On naming Cicely the winner, *The Challenge* remarked:

> The winning portrait by Miss C M Barker does, we think, give an excellent notion of the character of 'The Challenge' – its frankness, earnestness of purpose, determination, honesty - and youth!

Her prize-winning portrait for The Challenge *competition.*

During the years of the First World War her correspondence tutor, Alice B Woodward, helped Cicely fine-tune her watercolours for post-cards for J Salmon Art Publishers, C W Faulkner & Co, S Harvey Fine Art Publishers and the SPCK (the Society for Promoting Christian Knowledge). She gave advice on using colours (bearing in mind how they were likely to reproduce) and, in particular, on composition. She also urged Cicely to study from life, and to resist imitating commercial formulas. She stated in one of her letters:

> Everything one does should be done to the top of one's ability and the more one knows the less easily one is pleased with one's performances. Do you remember the verse in Kipling's 'Artistic Heaven', I think it is called [in fact, it is entitled 'When Earth's Last Picture is Painted']:
>
> *And only the Master shall praise us, and only the Master shall blame;*
> *And no one shall work for money, and no one shall work for fame,*
> *But each for the joy of the working, and each in his separate star,*
> *Shall draw the Thing as he sees It for the God of Things as They are.*

Although Cicely, with her strong Christian faith and sense of integrity,

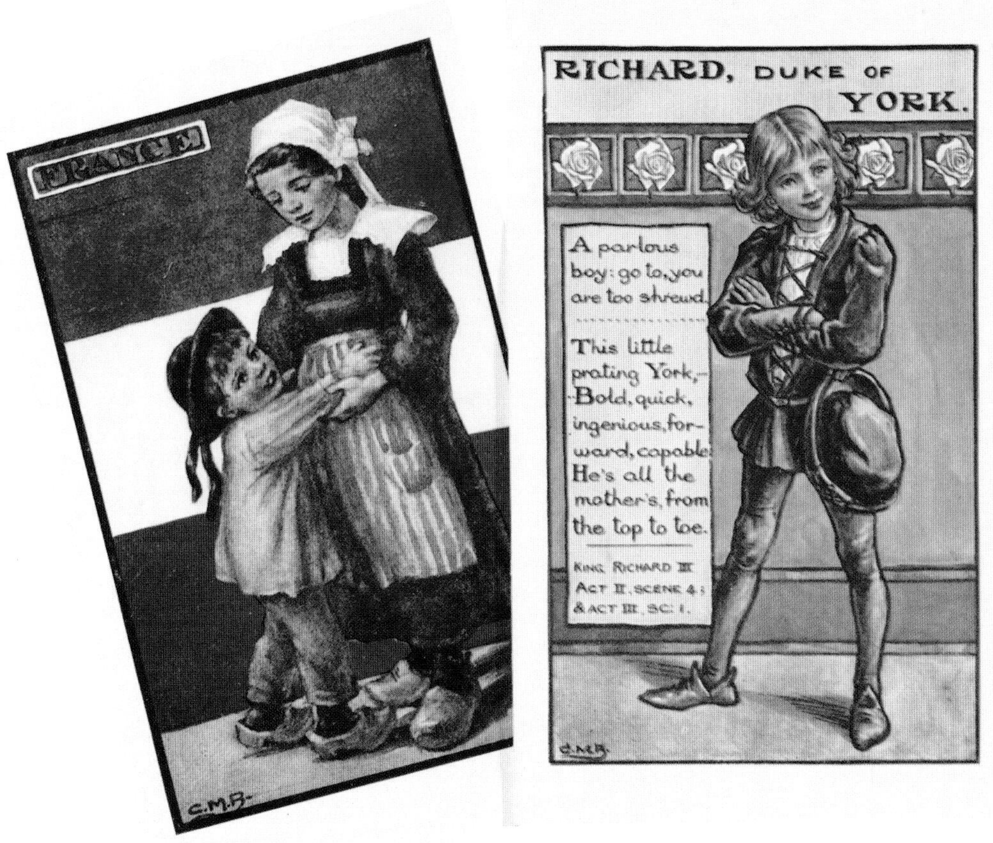

Examples of Cicely's commercial postcards.

would wholly have endorsed the sentiment of this poem, it must have been difficult for her to pursue what might have seemed selfishly high artistic goals when money was so short. But Alice B Woodward also reminded her:

> Remember also I give you rules and precepts . . . to help you during the time you are struggling to find out the right way for *you* to work – everybody's right way is their own.

Cicely's friend, Anne L Faulkner reiterated this advice. She comments on receipt of a set of Cicely's postcards: 'Do not follow *anybody's* way but your own! Keep to your dreams.'

In fact, Cicely was constantly receiving such advice in the early part of her career. Dr C W Philpot, a friend of the family, urged her to ignore the comment in the *Evening Standard* that her painting was 'out-of-date'. He wrote in a letter dated 24 October 1920: 'It shows imagination and originality of thought – the most precious things in art.' He goes on to quote Dante: '"If thou follow thy star thou canst not fail of glorious heaven." And your star is your own individual power of thought and imagination – the thread of gold that goes through all good art.'

Her cousin, Winnie Denham, sent her an extract pertaining to Edward Burne-Jones from *My Life and Some Letters* by Mrs Patrick Campbell. It reads:

> I have a valued letter from 'Dearest' giving me the fruits of his philosophy, saying he did not waste precious life on reading what the critics said, and that to real artists only one critic mattered – 'one's own savage, bitter self'.

Cicely admired the spirit of his work greatly. For Christmas 1920, her mother gave her the two-volume set *Memorials of Edward Burne-Jones* by his wife, Georgiana Burne-Jones. Cicely cherished these books, and kept pertinent cuttings within their pages. One of them is a review of Burne-Jones's life and work by Stanley Baldwin, his nephew. In it he quotes Burne-Jones as saying: 'I need nothing but my hands and my brain to fashion myself a world to live in that nothing can disturb. In my own land I am king of it.'

Cicely's friends and relations need not have feared that she would be distracted from her true course, for she shared with Burne-Jones the facility for creating her own world. Distanced from the demands of outside society by her protective family, she was free to live according to her own perception of the world. And it was a world in which children played an important part until her sister closed down the kindergarten in 1940.

Cicely could understand children because, in many ways, she retained the character of a child herself. She had a gentle and kind disposition, an enquiring mind and a thoughtful temperament, and she was born into a caring and Christian environment. She endured both physical and emotional suffering as a child and teenager, which served to strengthen her Christian faith and appreciation of the beauty of nature in plants, animals and humanity. She was grateful for her gifts as an artist and sought to improve them.

In her work she seemed to be following two precepts John Ruskin expressed in *Modern Painters* (Vols 1–5 published 1843–60). He believed that minuteness of handling and complete naturalism were essential; and great art ought to serve a high moral or spiritual purpose.

Drawings of children
from Cicely's sketchbooks.

The charm of Cicely's work reflects her own nature. Violet Clayton Calthrop commented admiringly in a letter to Dr Philpot, dated 17 April 1925, about *Flower Fairies of the Spring*: 'She has such exquisite *taste*, besides draughtsmanship.' And A Walford (a teacher at Woodford School) wrote to Dorothy: 'I was so pleased to see Cis, I think she has a beautiful face with a radiant soul shining out, it was a pleasure to look at her.'

Although other-worldly, Cicely was also determined. She sent her flower fairy paintings to several publishers before Blackie accepted them for publication in 1923. Bessie Watkins wrote to her: 'How nice that Blackie accepted your book, but I think the other publishers were very short-sighted to refuse it.'

She received only £25 for a total of twenty-four illustrations and verses for *Flower Fairies of the Spring*, but on completion of the sequel, *Flower Fairies of the Summer*, her mother wrote to Blackie suggesting that both books (and any further volumes) should attract a royalty. Blackie agreed.

Cicely was aware she owed much to her mother. She presented a copy of the first edition of *Flower Fairies of the Spring* to her mother, in which she had written the following rhymically faltering, symbolically over-obvious, but respectfully loving poem:

To Mother
This tiny cup of first fruit wine,
I call it mine,
But it is yours.
And why - because
You are the vine,
And I am yours,
And this is mine.
Thus, tendril-like, the words entwine,
The vine, the wine,
The 'mine', the 'yours',
Yet in one world they do combine,
– I and my vintage,
all are THINE.

With love from Cis
September, 1923

Cicely as a young woman.

First editions of the Flower Fairies books. The printed paper cases were protected by dust jackets of slightly different designs (above right).

Cicely's cousin, Winnie Denham, revealed the close nature of Cicely's and her mother's relationship when she wrote to her aunt Mary in 1954. 'I could never forget how Cis suffered when you were first so very sad and heartbroken when Uncle Walter died – she cannot be happy unless you are as happy as you may be.'

To her sister Cicely also acknowledged a debt. In the copy of *Flower Fairies of the Spring* she presented to Dorothy she inscribed a less emotionally wrought poem:

Croham Hurst in Surrey, one of Cicely's favourite places for sketching flowers.

To DOB
By hedge and footpath, Hills and Hurst,
Ere modern change had wrought its worst,
Went you and I on Saturdays,
And learnt the flowers and their ways.
To you, best Teacher, do I owe
The seed from which these fairies grow;
Take then this Little Book the First
Sprung from old lanes and fields and Hurst.

In 1924, Mary, Dorothy and Cicely moved to 23 The Waldrons, a three-storeyed, semi-detached Victorian house. They lived frugally, determined to keep up appearances despite their greatly reduced circumstances. Dorothy taught her young charges every morning in the back room and in the garden, weather permitting. Cicely painted in the afternoons in the specially-constructed studio in the garden, where her young models often complained of the cold. It was here that virtually all Cicely's work was done – whether for Blackie, magazines, religious societies or churches – for it was where she spent much of her life.

All three women attended church regularly – at St Andrew's and at St Edmund's. They did not care for the 'high' parish church but preferred to attend the 'low', which the less privileged attended. Just as she painted the children in Dorothy's kindergarten, Cicely included portraits of many of the church-goers in her religious works, using the same naturalistic approach as in her secular work. She sometimes worried that she was not doing enough for the church and in the late 1920s in a letter to her cousin and close friend, Winnie Denham, wondered if she should concentrate entirely on religious works. Winnie replied:

Cicely (left) with her mother and Dorothy in the garden at 23 The Waldrons.

I cannot gather entirely what is in your mind about your vocation – I do see that you are wanting not to go on just doing children's illustrations and no doubt you have lots of ideas budding – but it seems to me to get awkward when one begins to think of 'doing good' with that sort of work – you talk of things being 'merely clever' but I don't feel sure what does more good than really good and *beautiful* work. Of course, you might be clever and *wicked* and incite people to evil by stirring up evil ideas – but is that likely? It would seem a pity to me to devote all your time to religious themes – to put it baldly – . . . you naturally do good I should think by presenting anything *you* do to the public eye. But I do think you ought to be able to do what you feel impelled to do – not just what the publishers demand . . . But when all is said I don't think you would do *more* good by *limiting* your doings to religious subjects.

Winnie must have allayed her fears, for Cicely continued both strands of her work.

All through the 20s, 30s and 40s she continued to attend evening classes at Croydon Art School, finally teaching there. She made many friends for, as Winnie once commented to her, she was 'the most excellent, stimulating, companionable, improving and sympathetic friend'. She went on many sketching holidays with friends and family to Storrington and Amberley in Sussex, to the south coast, and Cornwall. She stayed with fellow artist Margaret Tarrant in Gomshall, Surrey, with Winnie in Sussex, with her cousin Kenny Oswald and his wife in Ugglebarnby, Yorkshire, and with her friend Edith Major at her country home near Storrington – 'Bartons'.

Although Cicely and Dorothy worked together on the book of Bible stories *He Leadeth Me*, for which Dorothy provided all the text, and also on *Our Darling's First Book*, there the collaboration ended. Cicely often wondered why Dorothy did not confide in her, but perhaps the following note from Cicely to their mother in the 1940s reveals the source of the problem. It reads:

Cicely picnicking with her friend Margaret Tarrant, captioned 'Miss Margaret Tarrant (in hat)'.

> Dearest old Mother
> All is well old dear. I expect Dot will report about kitchen matters.

It is perhaps not surprising that she was closer to her cousin and her artistic friends than to her sister, for it was Dorothy who managed the household, earned a steady income, and looked after both Mary and Cicely. In 1940 the live-in maid retired and Dorothy closed the school and did all the household chores herself. She allowed Cicely the freedom to concentrate on her art, which flourished, and which gained her many admirers from around the world.

Cicely probably did not realize how much she owed her sister until Dorothy's death (of a heart attack) in 1954, after which Cicely was unable to work, having herself to look after her mother – now in her eighties – and do

A cottage at Amberley, Sussex.

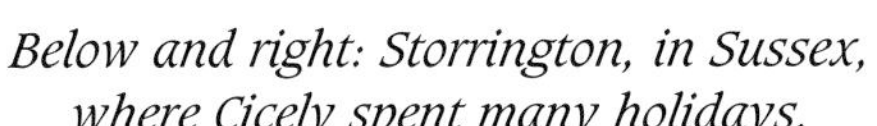

Below and right: Storrington, in Sussex, where Cicely spent many holidays.

'Bartons' near Storrington, the home of Cicely's friend, Edith Major, sketched in May 1928.

all the household chores. She did not even manage to complete the design for the stained-glass window in St Edmund's in memory of her sister until after her mother's death.

Cicely's mother died in 1960, and in 1961 Cicely moved from 23 The Waldrons into another house in Croydon, 6 Duppas Avenue. Her friend, Edith Major, had also died, and in her will left Cicely her small bungalow called 'Bartons', near Storrington in Sussex. Cicely had always wanted to live in the country and in 1961 she set about improving the state of the building, which had fallen into disrepair. She wrote to her cousin Kenny Oswald, telling him that she intended to rename the house 'Hareswith Cottage' or 'Hareswith Studio' as Hareswith was the local name. She used the name in her story *Simon the Swan*.

However, she never took up full residence there, finding its position isolated and the traffic on the narrow lanes rather daunting for an elderly woman with failing health. In December 1968, after a month in hospital, she wrote to tell another cousin, Tom Barker, 'I am planning to move away to Storrington where life should be more restful... I am buying the lease of a nice little maisonette there, quite in the midst of things – church and shops all handy.' She named her new home 'St Andrew's', revealing how much her local church in Croydon had meant to her.

From the time of her move to Storrington until her death in Worthing Hospital in February 1973, Cicely's health deteriorated and she spent extended bouts in nursing and convalescent homes. Her cousins Kenny Oswald and Tom Barker looked after her affairs and tried, like her helper Annie Hawkins, to make her old age reasonably comfortable. Perhaps because of her ill health as a child, she viewed her physical deterioration with good-humoured stoicism. She wrote to Tom and his wife Charmian from the convalescent home in Worthing on Easter Sunday 1970:

> I don't understand television. (I wish someone would just shout at me and tell me what place or person it is we are looking at.) I'm too blind and deaf.

Cicely in later life.

Her mind was just as enquiring as ever, though, for she continued:

> I wonder whether the New English Bible has anything different, in the beginning of St John's Gospel, for 'Without him was not anything made that was made'. I find myself thinking of that, when I study a daffodil for instance.

Finally, despite her extremely poor sight, she could still distinguish individual flowers. She wrote:

> It is getting quite flowery here. I am seeing more of 'Iris Stylosa' than I have ever seen before, silky pale mauve ones, and quite dark blue-purple ones, and hyacinths are out, in the front garden here, blue and pink ones.

So much of her nature is contained within this one letter. The obituary given on 16 February 1973 in *Outlook* magazine – the journal of Croydon Parish, – summarizes her character beautifully:

CMB, as she signed herself, has been described as a unique personality – friends will long remember her gentle kindness, her unworldly viewpoint, and delightful sense of humour. Hers was a life of courage, earnest endeavour and strong faith. At the last she bore any disabilities with Christian fortitude.

Cicely's ashes were scattered in 'the glade' at Storrington churchyard. Eleanor Harwood-Matthews, her friend in later years, wrote after her funeral on 1 March 1973:

> The two services [one at Storrington church, the other at her home 'St Andrew's'] were so peaceful and lovely – just as she would have liked it – so like herself.

The beauty of her character and the scope of her talent remain for all to see in her work.

A view of Storrington, where Cicely spent the last years of her life.

Flower Fairy Paintings

When Walter Blackie published *Flower Fairies of the Spring* in 1923, the subject of fairies was very much in the public mind. Only the previous year, Sir Arthur Conan Doyle's book *The Coming of the Fairies* was published, giving an enormous boost to a belief in their existence. It prompted Margaret Tarrant (later a close friend of Cicely's) to paint *Do you believe in fairies?* for the Medici Society in 1922. Conan Doyle's book contained five photographs of fairies taken between 1917 and 1920 by two girls, Elsie Wright and her cousin Frances Griffiths, at a place known as Cottingley Glen just beyond the Wrights' garden. The photographs had been declared authentic by expert photographer H Snelling, and Conan Doyle was convinced they were genuine. It was not until the mid-1980s that they were proved beyond doubt to be fakes, and their originators finally admitted that the fairies were in fact cardboard cut-outs (although Frances maintained to her death that the fifth photograph was of a real fairy bower). In all probability, Elsie based the cardboard fairies in the first photograph on an illustration by Claude A Shepperson that appeared alongside a poem by Alfred Noyes called 'A Spell for a Fairy' in *Princess Mary's Gift Book*, published in 1915.

Margaret Tarrant's painting,
Do you believe in fairies?

Queen Mary did much to encourage the vogue for fairy painting during the 1920s by frequently sending postcards depicting fairies to her friends. She was a particular admirer of the work of Ida Rentoul Outhwaite (1889-1961), an Australian, whose illustrations received widespread acclaim with the publication there in 1916 of *Elves and Fairies*. In England A & C Black published many of her subsequent books, all with fairy themes, and also issued many of her illustrations as postcards. Cicely must have been aware of her charming work, and perhaps it was this artist who inspired Cicely to depict her own elves and fairies in a set of six postcards published by S Harvey Fine Art Publishers, in 1918.

Of course, fairy painting was nothing new. The Victorians, in their desperation to retain a sense of the spiritual in an age of ever-increasing industrialization and growing dependence on scientific fact turned to a Utopian fairyland for reassurance. Thousands of people were physically uprooted from the countryside where their families had lived for generations in close-knit communities, to live and work in the fast-growing towns and cities in polluted, overcrowded and totally alienating conditions. Suddenly they were living in an era in which everything could be explained by reason, and science was the basis of all fact. Imagination had no part to play amid the machinery and materialism of this world, so many painters turned to the past, to the time of Shakespeare, when magic was part of everyday rural life, when belief in the fantastic was acceptable, and they made the imaginary world tangible by painting forms of fairyland for everyone to see. Thus they maintained a link with a more superstitious and spiritual past. Sir Joseph Noel Paton was an exponent of such art. He, like many others, took Shakespeare's *A Midsummer Night's Dream* as his inspiration to create two works – *The Reconciliation of Oberon and Titania* (1847) and *The Quarrel of Oberon and Titania* (1849). The fairy people in these paintings seem more real than the human ones, being possessed of the whole gamut of human emotions and impulses.

Fairy stories and folk tales collected by the Brothers Grimm were published between 1823 and 1826, and in 1846 tales from Denmark retold by Hans Christian Andersen appeared, illustrated by George Cruikshank. William Blake claimed to have seen a 'fairy funeral' in his garden, and many established authors tried their hands at fairy stories. John Ruskin, who in a letter to Kate Greenaway asked 'Do you believe in fairies?', wrote *The King of the Golden River* (1851); and Thackeray, using the pseudonym 'M A Titmarsh', wrote *The Rose and the Ring* (1855). Both are fairy stories. Disturbing fantasy worlds were created by Christina Rossetti (whose poems were a particular favourite of Cicely's) in *Goblin Market* (1862), and by Lewis Carroll in *Alice's Adventures in Wonderland* (1865) and *Through the Looking Glass* (1871), both illustrated by Sir John Tenniel.

By the mid-1800s it was deemed acceptable to write books for children that set out primarily to entertain. (Until that time only instructional books were approved of.) Charles Dickens maintained in 'Frauds on the Fairies' that 'in a utilitarian age, of all other times, it is a matter of grave importance that fairy tales should be respected'. Richard Doyle's

Sir Joseph Noel Paton's The Reconciliation of Oberon and Titania.

illustrations to *In Fairyland* by W Allingham (1870) have a specifically mischievous and highly active quality about them which children must have enjoyed. And Walter Crane declared in the 1860s that 'the best of designing for children is that the imagination and fancy may be let loose and roam freely'.

Whether depicted for adults or children, fairies and elves were always in a pastoral setting. They were part of the natural world that was at once real and other-worldly. The flowers, trees, grass and animals were depicted in loving detail, and the fairy folk interacted with the natural elements, sheltering under nodding flower heads, leaning or sitting on toadstools. Children were admitted to this fairyland, this dream world, as they did not yet possess the cynicism of reason and the mistrust of the imagination. Thus the child in *The Elf Ring* by Kate Greenaway is able to commune with the elves, to become part of their moonlit circle in the depths of the forest of the subconscious.

It was only children, too – Wendy, John and Michael – who were able to gain entrance with Peter Pan to the Never Never Land in J M Barrie's play *Peter Pan* (performed at the Duke of York's Theatre in 1904) and books – *Peter Pan in Kensington Gardens* (1906) and *Peter and Wendy* (1911). Barrie's creation struck a chord in the nation's heart. In 1908

Margaret Tarrant's celebrated painting, Peter's Friends.

Cicely was given a copy of *Peter Pan in Kensington Gardens* and must have pored over the wonderfully evocative illustrations by Arthur Rackham.

By the Edwardian age, people had grown sentimental; they now yearned for an age of innocence and simple truths; they wanted to escape the harsh realities of progress, and return to a mentally less taxing, more unified world. Margaret Tarrant's painting *Peter's Friends*, published in 1921 by the Medici Society, was incredibly popular. Two children gaze yearningly at a ring of fairies playing round the statue of Peter Pan erected in Kensington Gardens by Sir George Frampton in 1912.

When the play's run came to an end in January 1929, Cicely wrote a poem entitled 'Last Night of Peter Pan' which she sent to Jean Forbes-Robertson, the actress who played Peter. Although a rather poor poem, it sums up the sadness felt by many at what seemed the end of an era.

> *Intangible, elusive, gallant, gay;*
> *With limbs of superhuman boyish lightness;*
> *Lit from within by some mysterious brightness,*
> *And yet with tragedy not far away -*
> *All this you seemed; you held us through the play*
> *Entranced as though by moonlight's radiant whiteness,*
> *The very Peter, unsurpassed in rightness:*
> *And now the play is ended. Peter, stay!*

Arthur Rackham provided fifty illustrations for *Peter Pan in Kensington Gardens*. Although his images are firmly in the world of fantasy, he based his characters on real-life models and, like Cicely's, his friends and family appear repeatedly in his illustrations. He also kept a collection of costumes and props which he used. His imagery is often frightening but he felt that 'children will make no mistakes in the way of confusing the imaginative and symbolic with the actual' (*The Junior Book of Authors*). This sentiment is echoed by Cicely in the foreword of *Flower Fairies of the Wayside* (1948), where she states:

> So, let me say quite plainly, that I have drawn all the plants and flowers very carefully, from real ones; and everything that I have said about them is as true as I could make it. But I have never seen a fairy; the fairies and all about them are just 'pretend'. (It is nice to pretend about fairies.) Now, I think, children will be able to tell the true parts from the pretend parts in these books.

Cicely Mary Barker very much admired the Pre-Raphaelites and took to heart their tenet of 'truth to nature', by which they meant both truth to the particulars of the natural world, and truth to human nature – the emotional and spiritual world. The Pre-Raphaelite Brotherhood (formed in 1848 by John Everett Millais, William Holman Hunt and Gabriel Rossetti, and later joined by Burne-Jones) looked, in an industrial and scientific age, to the precursors of Raphael for inspiration. They painted

Autumn Leaves *by John Everett Millais.*

directly from nature, *en plein air*, as the early Italians had done, and they depicted nature in minute detail, maintaining enormous accuracy in its particulars. In this way, they lent the mystical a sense of reality.

Cicely stated in an interview given to the *Croydon Advertiser* in January 1964:

> I am to some extent influenced by [the Pre-Raphaelites] – not in any technical sense, but in the choice of subject matter and the feeling and atmosphere they could achieve. I very much like, for example, the early paintings of Millais and, though he is later, the wonderful things of Burne-Jones.

The Pre-Raphaelites were aligned to the Romantic movement of the eighteenth and nineteenth centuries. They sought a personal, passionate relationship with nature in an effort to capture a spirituality that had been lost with urbanization and the march of scientific knowledge. Millais' *Autumn Leaves* (1856) expresses both the poignancy of this loss in the burning of the perfectly delineated leaves and in the wistful expressions on the faces of the children, and the continuing belief in the holiness of nature in the glow of the twilight.

Cicely's family had owned the two-volume set, *The Life and Letters of Sir John Everett Millais* by John Guille Millais since 1899, and so she had had plenty of opportunity to study his beliefs and work. He was the most naturalistic of the group, and took great trouble with his depiction of plant life. For *Ophelia* (1851–52) he sat for hours by a stream near Ewell in Surrey studying the bank and the water. In addition, he examined the plants and flowers to be included, often with a magnifying glass. His model for the painting, Elizabeth Siddal, had to undergo some discomfort in the name of naturalism. He made her wear an old and dirty dress and lie for hours in a bath filled with water, which was kept warm by oil lamps set underneath it. She caught a severe cold as a result of this, and under threat of an action for £50 damages, Millais paid her doctor's bills.

Cicely also used real-life models for her paintings. Most of the models came from the kindergarten her sister Dorothy ran in the back room of the house in which they lived, but she also used the children of neighbours. Gladys Tidy, the girl who came in every Saturday to do household work, such as blackleading the stove, posed for six of the flower fairies. Clearly Cicely was very fond of Gladys, and often paid her 2d or 3d a sitting.

Gladys's daughter, Brenda Litchfield, later posed for the Blackberry Fairy (*Flower Fairies of the Autumn*), and recalls holding the prickly stem.

Cicely always made the child model hold the flower, twig or blossom of a particular fairy, for she wanted to be sure of the accuracy of her depiction of the shape, texture and form of the plant. Her only alteration was to the size, for she enlarged the flower to make it the same size as the child. In addition, just as Millais personally selected the dress – all flowered over in silver embroidery – for Elizabeth Siddal, to match his vision of Ophelia exactly, so Cicely created the costumes for her flower fairies. She kept the materials in a large chest in the studio in the garden, where she also kept wings made of twigs and gauze. For each flower fairy she made a new costume, meticulously unpicking the stitches of each one once the painting was finished, in

Gladys Tidy as the Primrose Fairy.

order to reuse the material. Cicely's grandmother, Eleanor Oswald, had given her a copy of Dion Clayton Calthrop's *English Costume* for her twenty-first birthday. She referred to this often when creating the costumes for the flower fairies.

Cicely's flowers are always botanically accurate. If she could not find the flower she wished to paint close at hand in the garden or growing wild, she referred to 'the beautiful series of books *Wild Flowers as they Grow*, by G Clarke Nuttall (Cassell)' (from the foreword of *Flower Fairies of the Wayside*). She copied descriptions given in these books into one of her notebooks, in which she also enclosed pertinent cuttings from the nature sections of newspapers, including pages from the *Santa Barbara Gardener* sent to her from America by her friend and admirer, Margaret Ely Webb. In addition, she enlisted the help of staff at Kew Gardens, to whom she sent specimens for identification, and whom she also thanks in the foreword. Indeed, Brenda Litchfield recalls that a man from Kew Gardens would call round to the house with specimens for her to paint. And her fairies are not ethereal fairies of the supernatural but portraits of real children, whose characters match the characters of the flowers.

By choosing to depict children, she echoed Wordsworth in many of the poems in *Lyrical Ballads* (1798-1800), and Blake in his *Songs of Innocence* (1789). They wrote of ordinary, rustic children whose spirituality shone through their innocence, whose natural impulses were as yet untempered by the rigours of convention and learning.

Cicely searched for a publisher for her flower fairy paintings and, in March 1922, Blackie accepted them, asking her to paint an additional eight flower fairies to complete the book. *Flower Fairies of the Spring* was published by Blackie in 1923. Although Cicely had chosen a subject that was seeing a revival of popularity with the play and books featuring Peter Pan, nevertheless her flower fairies were very much her own creation. It was the clever and charming interrelation of plant form and character with child form and character that friends and family to whom Cicely sent copies of her first flower fairy book so admired. Reviewers loved it too. B E Baughan encapsulated the response of many in his article for the *Otago Witness*, New Zealand, on 7 October 1924. He stated that:

> [The flower fairy paintings] interpret the spirit of each blossom in a way, and with a success, quite original. The imagination of the artist, one Cicely Mary Barker, has linked together three ideas of beauty, connected already in most of our minds, and has here embodied them in one. Flowers, children, fairies – how well they go together, and how skilfully she has proved they do, in each of these little pictures, wherein each flower is depicted as a fairy, and each fairy is depicted as a child.

> There is a very real art in all of them, for they give the essential 'truth' of each blossom in that heightened and blessed clearness that only imagination can supply.

There is a grace and delicacy of line and colour in the portrayal of both child fairy and flower. The outline pen work is fine and the poses natural. Margaret Tarrant's flower fairies are more stylized and less fluid than Cicely Mary Barker's. For example, the Poppy Fairy painted by Cicely for *Flower Fairies of the Summer* (published by Blackie in 1925), is far more naturalistic than Margaret Tarrant's 'Poppy' (C W Faulkner, 1909), which owes more to Art Nouveau and the Decorative Arts than to the Pre-Raphaelites. In Cicely's painting the fall of the rich orange-red dress, together with the ragged undulating hem and neckline, and the way the dress is loosely gathered together at the waist to form a ragged dark centre, perfectly reflect the form of the flowerhead. In addition, the varicoloured light wash of the background is just enough to suggest the changing colours of the wheatfield.

Flower Fairies of the Summer was published in 1925 and *Flower Fairies of the Autumn* in 1926. In *Autumn* Cicely had began to make her fairies play a more active role in the paintings, investing them with additional human traits and really making them part of the plant. The Beechnut Fairy is depicted mischievously throwing down the nuts from the tree, and the Horse Chestnut Fairy waits for the moment when he can shake down conkers on boys who often hit him in their efforts to knock them out of the tree.

In 1927 the three seasonal flower fairy books were published in a single volume entitled *The Book of the Flower Fairies*. For this volume Cicely provided a beautiful ink and wash endpaper design depicting a flower fairy from each season running across open fields. It marked the end of the first series of flower fairies. She returned to the subject to complete *A Flower Fairy Alphabet* (published by

Poppy Fairies, as depicted by Margaret Tarrant (above) and Cicely (below).

The Vetch Fairy comforts the unlucky U Fairy in A Flower Fairy Alphabet.

Blackie in 1934), and then left the theme until the 1940s when *Flower Fairies of the Trees*, *Flower Fairies of the Garden* and *Flower Fairies of the Wayside* were all published.

In *A Flower Fairy Alphabet*, Cicely both shows and describes a fairyland where a belief in Christian virtues is fundamental. Kindness and compassion (a sentiment that can be traced through all the Pre-Raphaelite painters) are beautifully illustrated by the fairy who protects the Apple Blossom baby from 'frost and blight', and by the Vetch Fairy, who rests a friendly hand round the shoulder of the U Fairy who 'hasn't a flower: not one', and offers to share all the V flowers with him. The sad and troubled look on the face of the U Fairy, together with the baby-like upward curling of his toes, creates a strong desire in the viewer, as well as in the Vetch Fairy, to look after him.

After completing her story book *The Lord of the Rushie River* in 1938, Cicely Mary Barker turned again to the theme of fairies with the first of her second set of three little books on the subject – *Flower Fairies of the Trees* (published by Blackie in 1940). During a time of upheaval and war people once again seemed to find an idyllic fairyland, where everything is ordered 'good and fair' and man is at one with nature, alluring and reassuring. It is remarkable that Cicely Mary Barker could create so charming and peaceful a fairy world in the middle of the Second World War. In fact, if it had not been for the devastation of the war she would have embarked on *Flower Fairies of the Garden* two years earlier, in September 1940, when her editor at Blackie first suggested the theme of garden flowers (together with butterfly fairies, toadstool fairies and, thinking no doubt of 'Digging for Victory', fairies of the vegetable garden). However, she was unable to work well at the time, much to her chagrin. She recorded in her workbook in December 1940: 'This has been a disgraceful year, with the small amount of work done, the only excuse is war and Air Raids. The studio skylight was broken on 17 October.'

In 1945 she began work on her last flower fairy book – *Flower Fairies of the Wayside* (published by Blackie in 1948). She recorded in her workbook:

> Mother and I were at Deal for a fortnight in September; and before we went, and while there, and when we came back, I was making studies for a new flower fairy book: *Flower Fairies of the Wayside*.

This reveals her characteristic way of working – first she made studies of the plants and children, often while on holiday in the country. She then completed the paintings in quick succession, and finally wrote the verses.

In 1950 Blackie published this second set of three flower fairy books in a single volume entitled *Fairies of the Flowers and Trees*. For the endpaper of this edition, Cicely Mary Barker provided a wonderful ink and wash design. Three fairies move in procession carrying blossom, flowers and fruit, while all around them, both flying at their shoulders and walking at their feet, proceed the flower fairies of these and the first three books. Although they are so small, each fairy and its flower can be easily identified. This flower fairy parade provides the perfect ending to the flower fairy series.

In 1985, twelve years after Cicely Mary Barker's death, Blackie reissued the whole flower fairies series in a different format. By extracting appropriate flower fairies from the seven existing books, they were able to compile a volume of *Flower Fairies of the Winter.* This new arrangement of eight titles, which now included a flower fairies book for every season of the year, proved extremely popular and the books continue to be published in that way today.

The endpaper design for the second flower fairy compendium, Fairies of the Flowers and Trees (1950).

FLOWER FAIRY PAINTINGS

Plates

Postcards from Cicely's Elves and Fairies *series. Above: 'A Happy Meeting'.*

'The Dance of the Fairies'.

'A Joy Ride'.

The Dandelion Fairy, from Flower Fairies of the Spring *(1923), reflects the colours and shapes of the plant down to the sepals at the end of his sleeves and the pom-poms on the tops of his shoes.*

In the painting of the Wood Sorrel Fairy, also from Spring, *child and plant work equally well together to create a feeling of delicacy. The line of the wings follows exactly the angle of the petals.*

The smiling Greater Knapweed Fairy from Flower Fairies of the Summer *(1925). The verse accompanying this poem explains that the knapweed is harmless, in spite of his prickly, thistle-like appearance.*

The Nightshade Fairy, from Summer, *has averted eyes and his hand is held up in a forbidding gesture, for he warns in his verse: 'My flowers you shall not pick, nor berries eat, for in them poison lies.'*

The Beechnut Fairy from Flower Fairies of the Autumn *(1926) is depicted mischievously throwing down nuts from the tree.*

Cicely's friend, Dr Philpot, praised Flower Fairies of the Autumn. *'You have gained facility and sureness in your drawing . . . witness the Mountain Ash Fairy [above] for the hands and the Beechnut Fairy for the little feet.'*

Above: kindness and compassion are illustrated by the fairy who protects the Apple Blossom baby from 'frost and blight' in A Flower Fairy Alphabet *(1934).*

Right: Cicely's sketch from life of a double daisy plant with her illustration for the Double Daisy Fairy.

30th MAY.
SIDMOUTH.

D
CMB
Double Daisy

The Queen of the Meadow Fairy from A Flower Fairy Alphabet. *The grace of her pose, her simple dress, and her colouring of light greens and browns allow her to blend beautifully with her habitat.*

The Lily-of-the-Valley Fairy from A Flower Fairy Alphabet. *The sketches below show the child model who posed for the picture and the flower study used as background.*

The Gorse Fairies from A Flower Fairy Alphabet *illustrate the old saying that when the flowers are in bloom, kissing is in fashion.*

The more mystical and sensual side of fairyland is epitomized by the Jasmine Fairy. In the heat of summer the 'cool green bowers' and 'sweet-scented' flowers are particularly seductive.

The Willow Fairy from Flower Fairies of the Trees *(1940). Her sylph-like form echoes the line of the long, slim leaves as she dips her toes in the stream.*

Cicely used her portrait of 'The Garden Boy' as the reference for the watchful Elm Fairy.

In the later books fairies often interact with wild creatures. Here a bee can be seen entering the mouth of the snapdragon in Flower Fairies of the Garden *(1944).*

The most charming paintings in Flower Fairies of the Garden *are the double portraits, like this one of the Polyanthus and Grape Hyacinth Fairies talking animatedly together.*

A Sweet Pea Fairy tries a flower bonnet on her young sister. The baby is supported by the wide leaf of the plant and one of its tendrils curls around her middle, making sure she does not fall.

Cicely almost always sketched the flower from life before she incorporated it into a fairy painting, as with this illustration of the Lavender Fairy from Flower Fairies of the Garden.

The Rose Fairy originally appeared in Flower Fairies of the Garden *but was transferred to* Flower Fairies of the Summer *in later editions. She is very much a part of her plant, leaning at the same angle as the stem.*

Cicely made detailed botanical studies of the bee orchis before she painted the Bee Orchis Fairy for Flower Fairies of the Wayside *(1948).*

The Ribwort Plantain Fairy whistles a tune to an alert-looking snail climbing up the stem of the plant in Flower Fairies of the Wayside.

Almost all the Wayside *fairies are active. The Tansy Fairy busies herself sewing her button-like yellow flowers on an elfin coat.*

An abiding image of fairyland as an inner world of dreams and desires is provided by the White Bindweed portrait from Flower Fairies of the Wayside.

PAINTINGS OF CHILDREN

Cicely Mary Barker sketched, painted and made pastel portraits of children all her life. Many she gave to friends, such as 'the two little drawings – baby, and boy in doublet and hose', which she drew directly into the albums of Rosie and Nelly Parsons (1922), daughters of 'Rose Bose', the cook; and the watercolour of 'little baby Alistair', which she gave to his mother after his death (July 1936). She also painted pastel portraits of her young cousins and gave them to their parents. For example, in 1951 she portrayed Martin and Ianthe Barker for their parents (her cousin Tom and his wife Charmian Barker); and in 1950 and 1963 she completed pastel portraits of her cousin Geoffrey Oswald's children, Nigel, Gordon and Juliet. She gave other portraits as Christmas presents, such as 'the six little heads on enamelled tin boxes' (1921). Some she donated to sales held by her sister Dorothy or her aunt Alice and to charitable or church-run institutions. Many she did for exhibitions – Royal Academy Summer Exhibitions, Croydon Art Society Exhibitions, the Pastel Society Exhibitions, the Women Artists' Exhibitions, and her own exhibition at the Craft House, Reigate, held in March/April 1939.

She always painted from studies done from life, whether at home or on holiday in the country or by the sea. In June 1936 she went to Amberley, Sussex, 'where I rented Stott's studio, and chiefly made studies of children. One head in oils of Flippence the garden boy, and others mostly in pastel.' The work she did here resulted in three pastel portraits, an oil painting and a charcoal drawing seen at the Croydon Art Society Exhibition in November 1936. One of the pastels – *Brown-eyed Lassie* (a portrait of June Cross) – was bought by the Croydon Corporation and it hung in Croydon library for many years. The oil portrait of Flippence, which she called *Country Boy*, was accepted for show at the Summer Exhibition in 1938, along with a watercolour sketch of a boy on a stile (Harold Chandler), which was also done at Amberley. Another of the pastel heads of June Cross done at Amberley was hung at the Women Artists' Exhibition in 1939. Cicely called the portrait *Summer Holidays*. The charcoal drawing of June, called *Little June*, was sold as a result of her successful exhibition at Reigate, where seventeen of the forty-two pictures and sketches were sold.

Of course, she also painted many children to commission. Her early postcards for Raphael Tuck, J Salmon Art Publishers and C W Faulkner & Co all featured children: *Picturesque Children of the Allies* (1915); *Seaside Holiday* postcards (1918 – redone in 1921 'when they changed hands' and published 1923); and *Shakespeare's Boy and Girl Characters* (1917, 1920). She illustrated stories and poems in magazines, such as *Child's Own* magazine; and she provided the illustrations for the covers and many of the stories inside the Blackie *Story Book* annuals throughout the 1920s and 1930s.

All the Blackie *Story Book* annuals were given titles featuring flora or fauna, so Cicely Mary Barker could combine her favourite subjects for painting – children and nature. The children in these illustrations are certainly romanticized and the countryside in which they reside is pretty and welcoming. The pictures as a whole represent an endless summer. The children's costumes are of all eras, but their poses are always naturalistic, and they fit perfectly in their country world.

Cicely Mary Barker also illustrated her own collections of rhymes, and her own stories. *Old Rhymes for All Times,* an anthology of verses, was published by Blackie in 1928. It was well received on publication. *The Inverness Courier* of 27 November 1928 commented on the 'special charm of personality' conveyed by the collection:

> . . . old as all the rhymes and fables are, she has spread a delicate glamour of her own over them all, and the love with which she regards them has added for us to their loveliness.

The Bookman of December 1928 calls the collection 'delightful', and goes on to say:

> The small black and white drawings dotted generously here and there and everywhere, which evince such a real sense of movement, alertness and expression, are equally as attractive as the full-page coloured plates whose imaginative charm and delicacy of treatment will make a strong appeal.

In conveying the emotions of children so well, Cicely Mary Barker must have been largely successful in fulfilling the wish expressed in the preface of her second poetry collection, *Rhymes New and Old* (published in 1933), that her pictures would entice children to read and learn. She states:

> They [the rhymes] range from traditional rhymes to names of famous poets, past and present; and if by introducing these names thus, in a

picture book, and in their most cheerful aspect, the door should be opened for any child to enter of his or her own accord into the world of English poetry, no higher result could be wished for.

Just as Walter Crane had taught children to read though visual stimulation in his alphabet books of the 1860s, so Cicely Mary Barker led children to a world of literature through her charming paintings of children, and she taught Christian morality and an understanding of nature in her choice of subject matter.

Compassion and Christian virtues can also be found in Cicely Mary Barker's first story of her own. In *The Lord of the Rushie River* (published by Blackie in 1938) Cicely creates a timeless, rustic world in which the child, Susan, is so much a part of the countryside in which she lives that she can understand the swans who live alongside her on the river. The swans, the ducks and the riverbank are all convincingly and endearingly drawn – from life – with characteristic ink outlines and pastel washes and are highly reminiscent of the Sussex countryside Cicely loved so much.

The delicate wash endpaper of Susan asleep on the swan's back, her

The endpaper design for The Lord of the Rushie River.

arms clasped around his neck, as he flies her home to Rushiebanks away from the town, has a dreamlike quality. It represents the inspiration for the story, which lay in a dream Cicely Mary Barker had as a child of flying on a swan's back, perhaps wanting to escape from the town to the countryside herself. She dedicated the book to 'Dear Miss Edith, with love', decorating the words with a whimsical line drawing of ducks. Edith Major was a good friend to Cicely all her life and was responsible for introducing her to the Sussex village of Storrington. Edith invited her to stay at her cottage, 'Bartons', which she was to visit again and again and which Edith later bequeathed to her.

A drawing from Cicely's 1944 sketchbook of the model for Princess Melina in Groundsel and Necklaces *(see page 90).*

It was at Storrington in December 1943 that Cicely 'wrote outlines of two stories for Blackie to choose from'. One was *Groundsel and Necklaces* (published by Blackie in 1946 and later retitled *The Fairy's Gift*, until published by Frederick Warne in 1991, when it became *The Fairy Necklaces*). The other was for *Simon the Swan* (published posthumously by Blackie in 1988). Blackie chose *Groundsel and Necklaces* and by July 1944 Cicely had written the story and 'made roughs for it'. She complains in her workbook that: 'It was difficult to get the story down to the length of *The Lord of the Rushie River* – in fact, with all my re-writing, it was still too long.' She continues: 'They are going to allow me an extra line of type on each page, and less pen drawings; but there are still some cuts to make.'

Although the fairies play an important role in *Groundsel and Necklaces*, providing Jenny with three hundred and sixty-five necklaces to enable her family to escape their life of poverty, the story and pictures transport us not to a fairy-tale world but to a very real one, set in about 1800, well before the industrial revolution. Cicely Mary Barker notes at the end of her synopsis:

> Costumes, I think, eighteenth or early nineteenth century. I imagine Mr Petercoo as a sort of pleasant Scrooge in appearance; a thin old man with knee-breeches and a tail-coat.

The story is one of social concerns, reminiscent of Charles Dickens in attitude and sentiment.

When composing the synopsis for the other story, *Simon the Swan,* in 1943, Cicely noted in her exercise book:

> Two real incidents helped to suggest this story. 1) In a small park near Croydon there was for a time a solitary swan on a small pond. The keeper told me he (the swan) had been found exhausted on the busy high-road outside; he was a young one, and the old couple on the larger piece of water would not let him come there. He looked sad and lonely, and eventually was taken to a pond in another park and provided with a mate. 2) I read in a newspaper about a swan who was accommodated on straw, and remained for two or three days, recovering and eventually flew away.

The actual story of *Simon the Swan* was not written until the early part of 1953. Cicely completed all the illustrations but Blackie did not publish the book until 1988, after her death.

The story is not so cohesive as either *The Lord of the Rushie River* or *Groundsel and Necklaces,* and it suffers from trying to combine the fairy-tale quality and natural setting of the first with the real-world quality and social setting of the second. Had Cicely written the story immediately after composing the synopsis in 1943, with *The Lord of the Rushie River* still relatively fresh in her mind, I believe the result would have been far more satisfying. She meant it as a sequel to *The Lord of the Rushie River,* but by 1953 she and the world had lost the gentle mood of 1936–7.

However, it is still a charming moral tale and the illustrations are delightful. Cicely's style had altered since the completion of *Groundsel and Necklaces.* The ink outlines were less emphatic in delineating the figures, and the background washes were more relaxed and impressionistic than earlier. The abiding impressions given by the illustrations for this book are of a love of nature and of the affinity of children with both the countryside and animals.

Paintings of Children

Plates

A portrait of three-year-old Ianthe Barker, painted in 1951.

A page from Cicely's 1938 sketchbook showing a drawing of young June Cross, whom she often used as a model.

'Japan', from the postcard set, Picturesque Children of the Allies *(1915). In this series each of the allied countries is represented by two or more children in traditional costume in front of the flag of their nation.*

Postcards from the Shakespeare's Boy and Girl Characters *series (1917 and 1920). Each card shows a single figure against a decorative background with a verse from the play which describes the character.*

CMB
Paddling.

Cicely's Seaside Holiday *postcards (1918), based on her sketches of children at the beach, are among the most charming of her cards depicting children.*

Left: a page from the sketchbook she took on holiday to Broadstairs in 1915 which shows figures used in the postcard 'Bathing' (above).

'The Telescope' has a cartoon quality about it, as an older girl frantically rushes to catch a small child who is running to the cliff edge. The lightness of touch, and easy delineation of movement and expression in these postcards are reminiscent of Caldecott's charming and slightly comical scenes.

'Looking for sea shells' has a more sombre atmosphere. Cicely based it on a photograph of herself as a child (below).

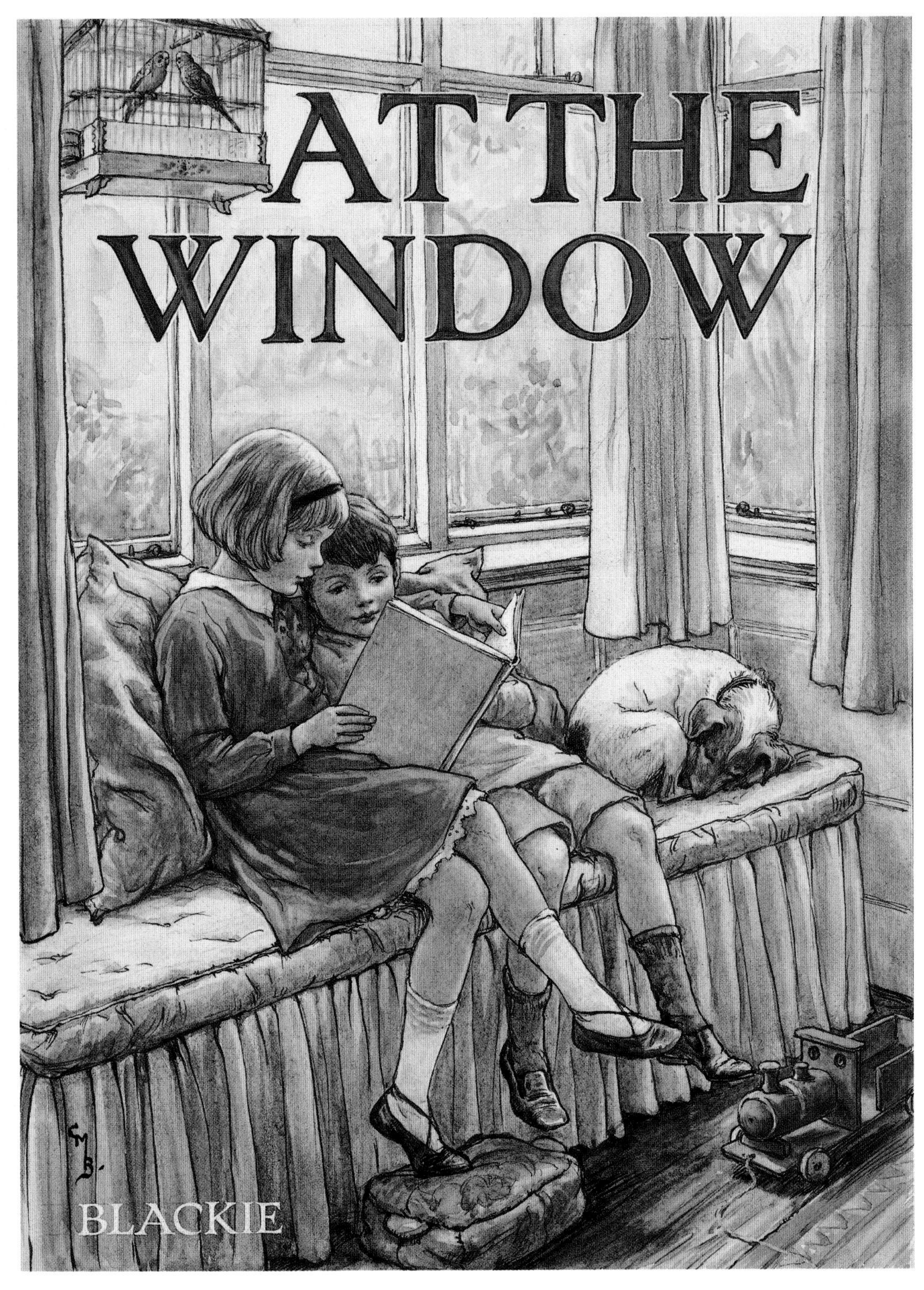

Above and right: front cover illustrations for Blackie books.

Cicely's book jackets usually depict two children sharing an activity or discovery.

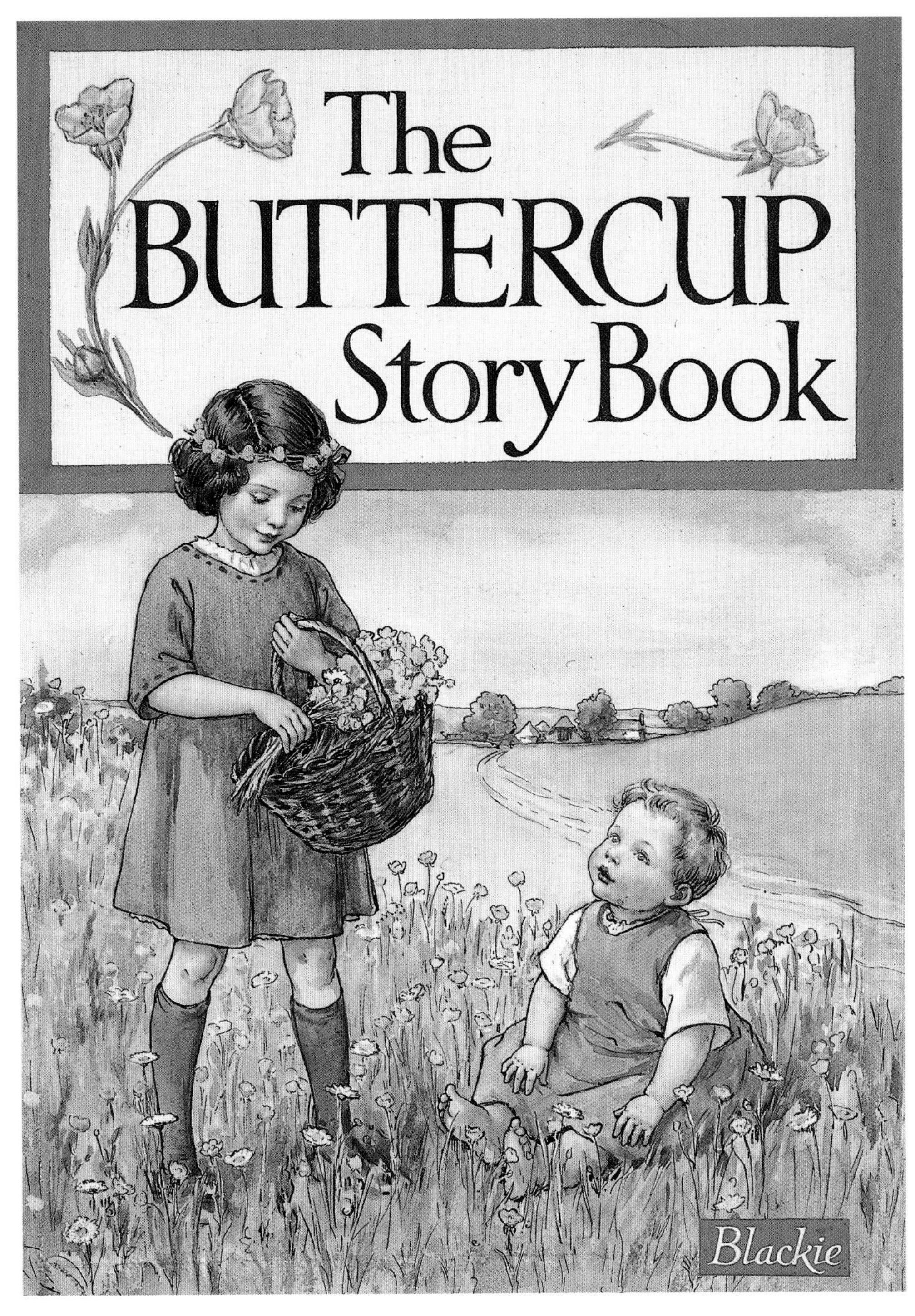

Blackie's Story Book *annuals usually have titles featuring flowers or birds and show children interacting with nature.*

An illustration for the rhyme 'About the Bush' in Old Rhymes for All Times *(1928), with two children in period costume.*

A touching illustration for Walter de la Mare's 'The Three Beggars' from Rhymes New and Old *(1933).*

The illustration for James Hogg's 'The Way for Billy and Me' from the same book shows a real companionship in the attitude of the two boys.

Above and right: two illustrations from The Lord of the Rushie River *(1938). The swan's raised wing and elegant curving neck convey his protective care for Susan.*

Father and daughter are reunited by the riverbank, with the encouragement of the swans and seagulls.

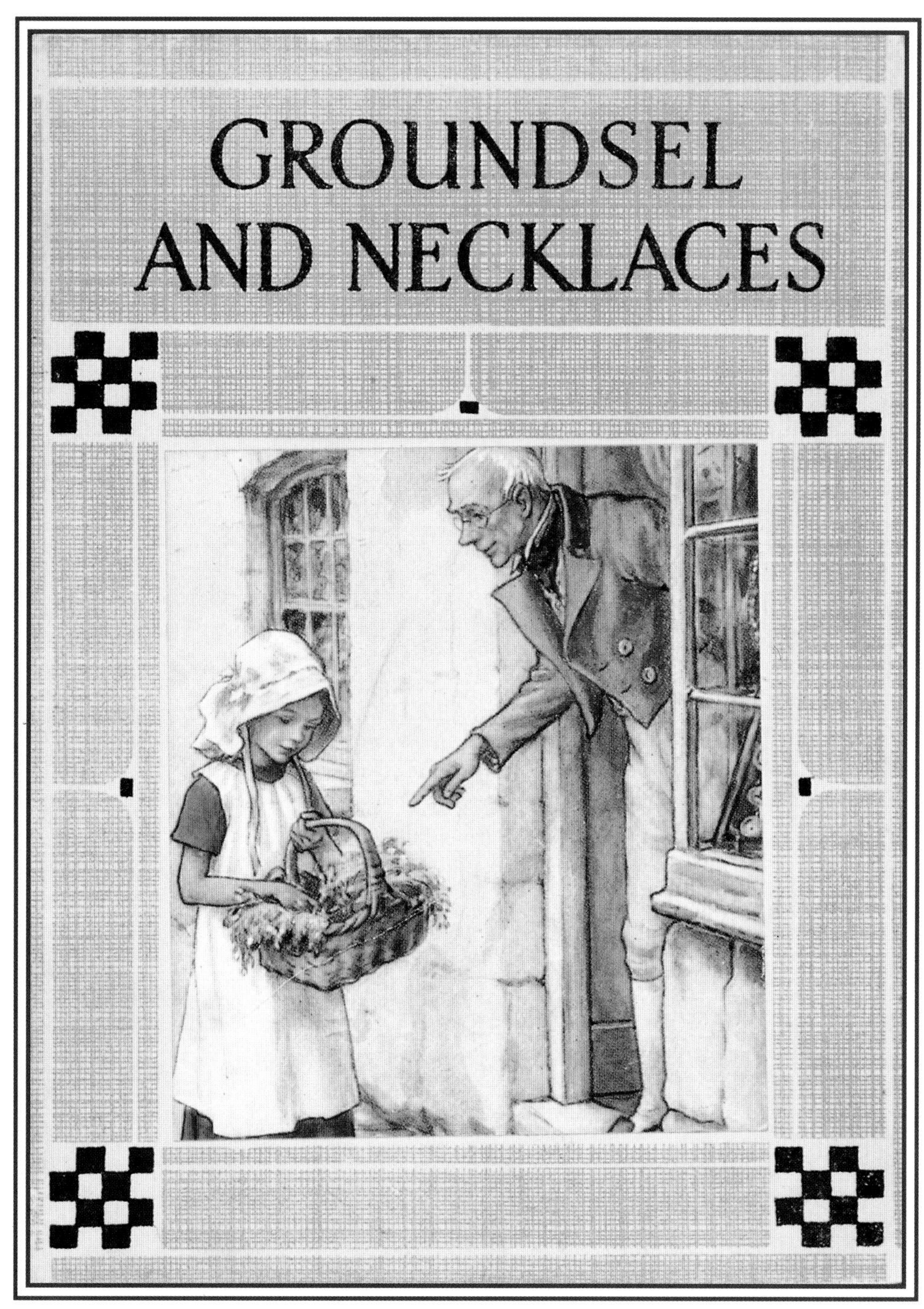

The front cover of the first edition of Groundsel and Necklaces *(1946), a story set in the early nineteenth century.*

'Too busy to take any notice', an illustration from Groundsel and Necklaces. *The composition very successfully conveys Jenny's sense of isolation in the crowd.*

Jenny meets the princess in Groundsel and Necklaces. *Jenny's costume for this important occasion resembles those worn by Kate Greenaway's characters.*

In this interior scene the figures are all turned inwards, drawing the eye to the box of necklaces in the centre.

An illustration from Simon the Swan *(first published 1988), showing the moment when Roger discovers he can talk to the animals.*

Religious Works

Cicely was a devout Christian all her life. Canon Ingram Hill remembers her as 'one of the pillars' of St Andrew's church. Indeed, the fellowship she found in this church must have meant a great deal to her, as she named her final home in Storrington after it. Her faith informed all of her work, religious or secular, whether in cards, children's books or decorating the churches with which she was affiliated.

As early as 1916 she designed a set of eight national mission postcards for the SPCK (the Society for Promoting Christian Knowledge), which she described as 'designed in about 10 days – dreadfully hurried'. The most successful of these is the illustration entitled 'Prayer' of a young woman (possibly modelled on her sister) kneeling in prayer before an open window. The light from outside falls on to the woman's face within, linking the work of God in nature with the innocent soul.

In 1923 she painted a series of five birthday cards featuring angels and babies, also for the SPCK. Taking the theme of the guardian angel, she composed a design for each year of a child's life from one to five. The children are again modelled from life: the one-year-old is portrayed by her cousin Geoffrey Oswald. Winnie Denham comments in a letter dated 29 December 1923: 'I daresay one year is *lovely* in the original – Geoffrey must be a darling'. The locations, too, are of places she had visited and sketched: the church in the five-year-old card shows the south porch at Beddington, near Croydon; and Winnie remarks, 'I think I like the three-year-old best – I think it must be the water near Waddon Mill'.

Cicely disagreed with the SPCK over elements of the birthday card designs. On the second they asked for a brambles-and-bryony background which she considered inappropriate, preferring flowers. She then had to make further alterations to the first and second designs. On the first she had to place a text on the wall rather than in the corner; and on the second she had to change the colour of the jersey sleeve of the child from emerald green to blue. This she clearly considered for the worst, writing in the workbook: 'Rotten, as I wanted the bright green.' Winnie Denham was probably right when she suggested in her letter that Cicely's 'part of the whole affair is on a totally different plane to the views of the Society, it seems to me – though no doubt they realize that themselves'.

In 1919 she designed the cover for the Society for the Propagation of the Gospel's (SPG) Peace Thank-offering booklet entitled 'A New Epiphany', the proceeds from the sale of which went towards the SPG's Peace Thank-offering Fund. The original painting was hung at the Croydon Art Society's exhibition of November 1919.

During the 1920s and 1930s and intermittently thereafter Cicely designed devotional Christmas cards for the Girls' Friendly Society (GFS). The first three that they bought in 1923 – all watercolours 9¼ x 5½ inches – sold out a combined edition of 46,500. Thereafter, the Society commissioned her virtually every year for almost two decades, providing her with the verses they wished her to illustrate. One such (1925) was a verse by Robert Herrick:

We see Him come, and know Him ours,
Who, with His sunshine and His showers,
Turns all the patient ground to flowers.
The Darling of the world is come;
And fit it is, we find a room
To welcome Him, the nobler part
Of all this house here, is the heart.

She describes it thus: 'the Christ Child standing, holding two Christmas roses, and with a border of the same flower and their leaves'.

The original watercolour for this particular card was bought by Queen Mary the following year. Cicely actually took the painting to Buckingham Palace, where she 'left it at the door'. She offered to make a gift of the painting to the Queen, but the Queen insisted on purchasing it. On receipt of the painting the following letter was sent from Buckingham Palace, dated 4 February 1926:

> Dear Madam, I am commanded by the queen to send you a cheque for £5.5.0 and to tell you how delighted Her Majesty is with your watercolour original 'The Darling of the World is come'. Excellent as the reproduction is, the original, of course, is far more attractive, and the Queen is very glad to possess so charming a picture.

Cicely also designed seven Christmas cards for an American publisher, Barton-Colton Inc, which all take the birth of Jesus as their theme. In one she depicts four children studying a model nativity scene in a church. Perhaps she based her design on the children's corner at St Andrew's church, where she mended the model repeatedly during the Second World War. In another she depicts the three wise men bringing gifts to the Christ-child, who – as any child would – reaches out to touch the shining gold.

She felt that the publisher spoiled two of the designs. In the first they had asked another artist to add Christmas fir with 'fairy lights' above the head of a blue-clad Mary holding the Christ-child in the cow-shed. This modern-day addition to the nativity scene jars horribly. She sent the card to her cousin Kenny and his wife, making it clear that the fir and lights were nothing to do with her. In addition, the publisher reproduced the verse written in her own hand, in bright red, to which she also objected. She wrote on the back of the card:

> The verse under the picture is reproduced from my rough lettering (in black, not red) which I never intended should be reproduced. I thought the verse would be printed in printer's type. I would have done it much more straight and neat if I had thought it would appear like this.

Two card designs 'embellished' by the publisher.

The other design changed was entitled 'Behold, I bring you good tidings of great joy', in which shepherds kneel before an angel, and another artist has added a border of fir and cones. Again, she sent the card to Kenny and Winnie, stating on the back: 'I am not responsible for the bits of limp fir tree; if I had known they were wanted, I might have supplied some better bits.'

Blackie commissioned her to do illustrations for two books with religious themes. The first, *The Children's Book of Hymns* (published in 1929 and, in 1933, reissued without the music as *The Little Picture Hymn Book*) arose out of an idea by Miss Margaret G Weed of Jacksonville, Florida, a Sunday school teacher, who felt that an illustrated collection of hymns for children was very much needed. Walter Blackie recorded in a note of 20 August 1930 that Miss Weed knew and liked Cicely Mary Barker's work and felt her to be 'pre-eminently well fitted to be a sympathetic illustrator of hymns. She accordingly made a special visit to this country to see Miss Barker and persuaded her to take on the task.' She must have visited in 1926, for Cicely records making sketches for 'an American Hymn Book' in May of that year. Two separate editions of the hymn book were published (the American in 1930), as the selection of hymns for America was different. Cicely Mary Barker received royalties on the English version, 'which met with a warm reception', and Miss Weed on the American, which was expected to be 'equally well received'.

In October 1933 Blackie commissioned Cicely Mary Barker to do sixteen three-colour illustrations, plus decorative line drawings, for a book of Bible stories published in 1936 as *He Leadeth Me*, which they asked her sister, Dorothy, to write. Cicely was delighted to collaborate with her (they shared the five per cent royalty), stating in her letter of acceptance to Blackie:

> I am very glad indeed that my sister is to write the stories; she is such a successful teacher of small children that I felt sure she could do it, but she is so modest about her own abilities that she would never have suggested it herself.

There were no more books with a religious theme for Blackie, although correspondence reveals that in the late 1940s, and again in 1952, Cicely considered 'The Little Book of Thanks'. However, although she was commissioned to do it, the book never came to fruition.

But she did provide several churches with works of art, from a copy of Madonna della Sedia done in oil on a noticeboard for the Mother's Union for a local church, St Edmund's church, Pitlake, (1920), to a design for a stained glass window for the same church in memory of her sister (1962). It was these works that she cared most passionately about.

In February 1922 she submitted a watercolour design for a cradle roll for St Edmund's in response to an advertisement in *Studio* by the Sunday School Union, which offered a prize for the winning entry. It measured 25 x 20 inches with spaces for 126 names, and was 'a design of our Lord blessing babies' and included an 'apple tree with blossom, and a lamb'. Her design was selected 'out of about fifty sent in' but they required her to make four alterations, one of which she objected to most strongly. She records in her workbook on 8 April 1922: '...worst, I had to take away the halo. Let it be put on record, *I had put a halo, I intended a halo, I wanted a halo*, *THE DESIGN NEEDED A HALO*.'

With this change, Cicely obviously felt that the integrity of the work was lost. Her will triumphed in the end, however. An entry in January 1923 states: 'Had the pleasure of adding halo to the copy of the Cradle Roll, for use at St Edmund's SS. It is not well reproduced [by lithography]; but I was able to make a few improvements besides the halo.'

Her next design for a church was a banner design for St Mary's church, Sanderstead, which was to be carried out in needlework. At the centre of the design was a figure of Mary, with the words 'My soul doth magnify the Lord', and the background suggested the hill country of Judaea.

Her first major church commission came in 1928 from her aunt, Alice Oswald, who was a head deaconess of the Church of England, and served mainly at the chapel at Llandaff House, Penarth, in South Wales, a house for destitute women. Cicely had supplied her aunt with paintings to sell to raise funds for this house (and continued to do so), and in 1920 her aunt had bought a watercolour (19 x 10½ inches) entitled *St Cecily's Garden* to hang in the chapel.

In February 1928, Cicely Mary Barker visited her aunt in Penarth, where she 'painted an inscription in black oil paint on a panel in the vestry of Auntie Alice's Chapel'. And it was probably during this visit that her aunt asked her to paint a triptych in oil for the altar of the chapel on the subject of *The Feeding of the Five Thousand*.

She began the studies and cartoons for the reredos in June 1928, and painted the panels (from left to right) over the course of the next nine months. In April 1929 she 'took the finished Reredos panels to Penarth, and saw them fitted'. They were dedicated by the Bishop of Monmouth on 25 April.

Her next major religious work was a triptych, again in oil, for the north wall of the chapel at St George's church, Waddon, (built in 1932) where Cicely and her sister taught at the Sunday school they founded there. Cicely began making studies and cartoons in August 1933. The design comprises a long central panel depicting *The Parable of the Great Supper* peopled with real 1930s characters, and two small outer panels – St John the Baptist on the left, Saint George the Martyr on the right. Cicely finished work on the triptych in November 1934. The picture was taken to the church in March 1935 and dedicated by the bishop on 17 March. The Parish magazine described the picture and event at length.

In 1941 Cicely painted individual pictures of the seven sacraments, in oil on smooth, fine canvas, to decorate the font of her local church, St Andrew's, South Croydon, where she was a regular worshipper. Later, she designed two baptismal rolls (one in 1948, the other in 1962), which decorate the wall behind the font. Both baptismal rolls are now filled with names.

In 1946 Cicely Mary Barker painted her greatest devotional work – for Norbury Methodist church. She entitled the oil painting (another panel, 4 x 7 feet) *Out of Great Tribulation*, and it was hung above the communion table in the Memorial chapel where it was dedicated on 10 July 1948. It is a highly emotive painting telling of hope rising out of sadness.

Cicely Mary Barker's final church contribution was made in her sixty-seventh year, to St Edmund's, Pitlake, in 1962, forty years after she had given them the cradle roll. She provided them with a design for a small stained glass window. It is a serene picture of a white-clad Christ carrying an earthenware bowl which he is about to fill with water from a pitcher in order to wash his disciples' feet. The window is captioned 'I am among you as he that serveth', and was Cicely's thank you to her devoted sister. The inscription underneath the window reads:

> To the Glory of God and in memory of Dorothy Oswald Barker 1893-1954 and her faithful work for this Church.

An SPCK postcard entitled 'Prayer' (1916). The model was probably Cicely's sister, Dorothy.

Religious Works

Plates

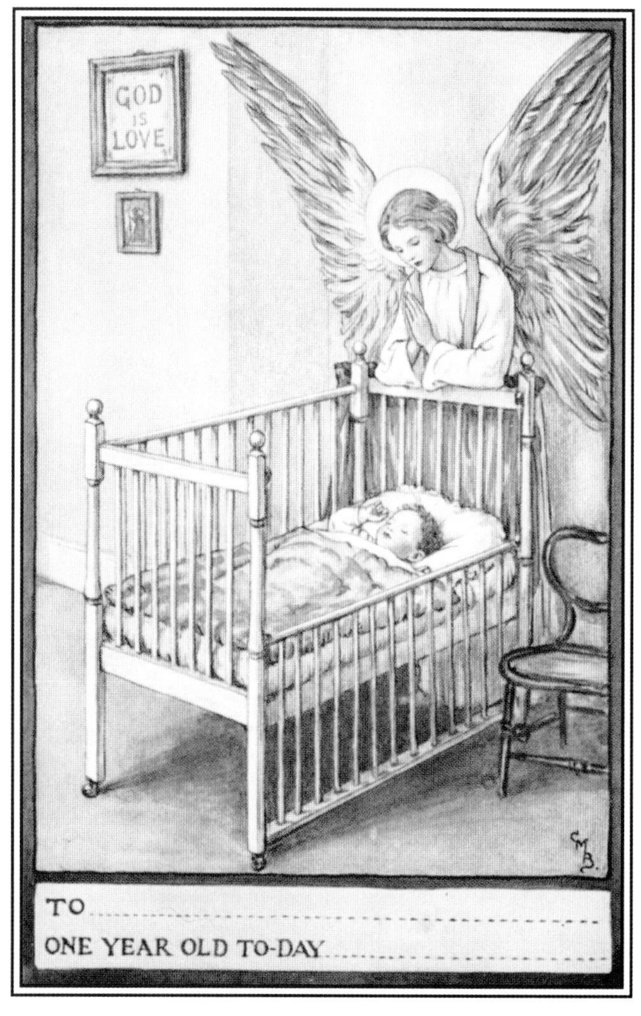

The first of the series of five Guardian Angel *birthday cards, published by the SPCK in 1923.*

For the second year card Cicely showed the guardian angel introducing the child to the natural world in the garden.

Cicely used naturalistic portraits and real locations in her religious works. The SPCK five-year-old card shows the church porch which she had sketched at Beddington (right).

The angels in the Guardian Angel *series bear a strong resemblance to those gathered round the four-poster bed in the picture with which Cicely illustrated 'Prayer at Bedtime' in* Old Rhymes for All Times, *several years later in 1928.*

Above: the cover for the SPG's Peace Thank-offering booklet entitled 'A New Epiphany' (1919).

Right: the GFS Christmas card 'The Darling of the world is come' (1925). The original watercolour of this card was bought by Queen Mary.

The 1932 GFS card, illustrating a verse by G K Chesterton. Mary tenderly leans over the Christ-child in a field of poppies, tulips and narcissi.

Cicely's design for the 1934 GFS card places Mary among a crowd of street children to illustrate the words by Richard Crashaw: 'Great little one, whose wondrous birth lifts earth to heaven, stoops heaven to earth.'

In the GFS Christmas card for 1936 Cicely portrayed the Christ-child alone in the darkness. The yellow light from the lantern reveals a beautiful, unafraid, trusting and upwards-looking young face.

A Christmas card design for the American publisher, Barton-Colton Inc, showing a model nativity scene. Cicely perhaps based this on the one in St Andrew's church, Croydon, which she was repeatedly called on to repair.

A Barton-Colton Christmas card depicting the three wise men bringing gifts to the Christ-child. The houses and deep blue sky of Palestine can be seen through the open door.

Above: an illustration for the hymn 'We plough the fields and scatter' from The Children's Book of Hymns *(1929).*

Right: Cicely's sketchbook contains a preliminary study for the boy with a sheaf of corn.

In the illustration for 'While shepherds watched their flocks by night' in The Children's Book of Hymns, *the angels dominate the picture; the spread wings of the seraph provide a canopy over the world which is relegated to the bottom quarter of the image and shrouded in darkness.*

The picture accompanying 'Onward, Christian Soldiers' is equally strong. Power is invested in the child warriors as they follow the path of God and the line of the spear-like flag-poles leads the eye towards the golden cross of Christ. The shimmering saints are present as a guiding force.

A serene and visionary picture illustrating the hymn 'I love to hear the story'. The little Western girl in the foreground looks up from her book to see the form of Christ surrounded by Middle Eastern children.

'The finding of Moses', one of the Bible stories from He Leadeth Me *(1936). Cicely had never visited Palestine and often found it difficult to make the faces look authentic. However, the figures are always convincing and the expressions telling.*

'Rhoda opened the door to Peter' from He Leadeth Me. *In this picture Cicely has captured the feelings of the characters - the maid's amazement, the man's scepticism, Peter's haste and anxiety - as well as an authentic lighting and setting.*

Cicely's watercolour painting of 'St Cecily's Garden' (1920) which her aunt, deaconess Alice Oswald, bought for the chapel at Llandaff House, Penarth, South Wales. It had previously been exhibited by the Old Dudley Art Society and singled out for praise in an Evening Standard *review.*

HE GAVE THANKS, AND BRAKE... AND

GAVE
TO HIS

The Penarth panel painting, 'The Feeding of the Five Thousand ', which was commissioned from Cicely by her aunt, deaconess Alice Oswald in 1928. The central panel shows Christ blessing the bread while two children wait at his feet, and the symmetrical side panels show his disciples distributing the bread to a subdued and seated multitude. It is not known what happened to this painting and the above black and white photograph, dating back to 1929, is thought to be the only reproduction of it in existence.

'The Parable of the Great Supper' in St George's church, Waddon (1934). The composition illustrates the verse from Luke 14 which is inscribed beneath the picture: 'Bring in hither the poor and the maimed and the halt and the blind'. The viewers of the 1930s would have recognized most of the figures in the central image, who were local people. Cicely even included her mother, who sits at the centre of the long table, and her dog, who stands in the foreground towards the left of the image. The intermingling of real characters with figures of adult angels showing people to their places, and child angels welcoming them, together with Christ presiding, has the effect of giving the mystical a sense of reality and follows exactly in the footsteps of the Pre-Raphaelites, who often used friends and relatives as models in images of medieval romance. The palette of luminous rusts, olives and ochres she favoured in such oil paintings are also highly reminiscent of the Pre-Raphaelites' colours. Cicely's use of oils in her church commissions imbued these works with a solidity and solemnity befitting the subject matter and setting.

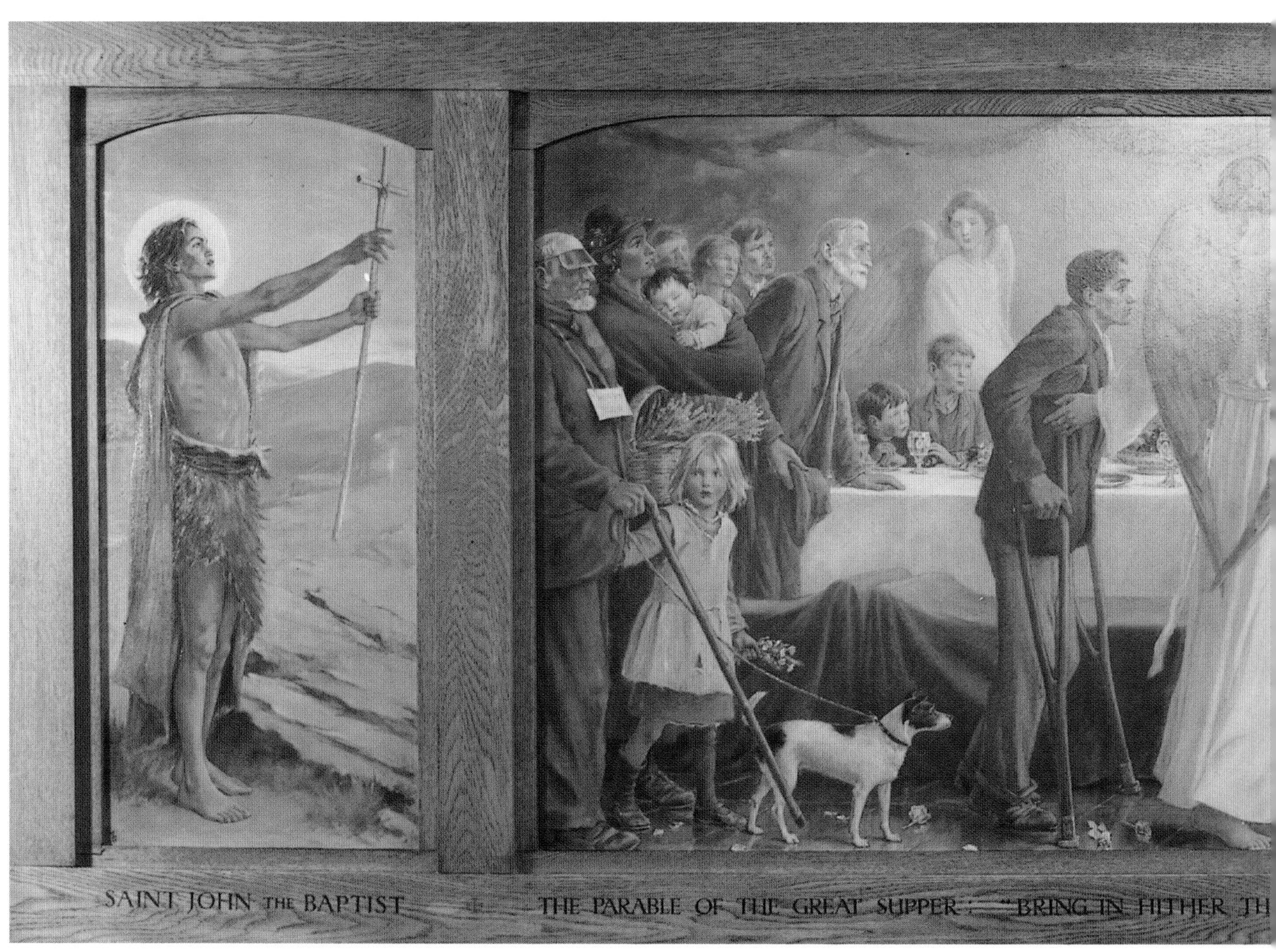

Left: Cicely did careful background studies of the roses scattered on the floor in front of the table.

'Out of Great Tribulation', painted for Norbury Methodist church in 1946, a highly emotive painting representing hope rising from sadness. Once again Cicely combines naturalism with symbolism and the figures in the crowd surrounding Christ are taken from real life. Her mother features again, to the right of the Christ figure. Some of the crowd are civilians but most are servicemen and women, accurately depicted in 1940s' uniforms, many of whom have suffered visible injury during the war.

Above: one of the font panels Cicely painted for St Andrew's church, Croydon, in 1941. She used her fellow worshippers as models and Canon Ingram Hill appears as the curate.

Right: the stained glass window Cicely designed in 1962 for St Edmund's, Pitlake, in memory of her sister Dorothy.

One of the baptismal rolls (painted by Cicely in 1948) which decorate the wall behind the font at St Andrew's church, Croydon. It is now filled with names.

LIST OF CICELY MARY BARKER'S BOOKS AND OTHER WORKS

CARDS	*Publisher*	*Date*
Picturesque Children of the Allies	J Salmon	1915
National Mission	SPCK	1916
Shakespeare's Boy Characters	C W Faulkner	1917
Shakespeare's Girl Characters	C W Faulkner	1920
Seaside Holiday	J Salmon	1918, 1921
Elves and Fairies	S Harvey	1918
Guardian Angel	SPCK	1923
Christmas cards	GFS	1920s, 1930s
Christmas cards (US)	Barton-Colton	1920s, 1930s
Beautiful Bible Pictures	Blackie	1932

BOOK ILLUSTRATIONS		
Annual (4 drawings)	Raphael Tuck	1911
Flower Fairies of the Spring	Blackie	1923
Spring Songs with Music	Blackie	1923
Flower Fairies of the Summer	Blackie	1925
Child Thoughts in Picture and Verse (M K Westcott)	Blackie	1925
Flower Fairies of the Autumn	Blackie	1926
Summer Songs with Music	Blackie	1926
The Book of the Flower Fairies	Blackie	1927
Autumn Songs with Music	Blackie	1927
Old Rhymes for All Times	Blackie	1928
The Children's Book of Hymns	Blackie	1929
Our Darling's First Book	Blackie	1929
The Little Picture Hymn Book	Blackie	1933
Rhymes New and Old	Blackie	1933
A Flower Fairy Alphabet	Blackie	1934
A Little Book of Old Rhymes	Blackie	1936
He Leadeth Me (Dorothy Barker)	Blackie	1936
A Little Book of Rhymes New and Old	Blackie	1937
The Lord of the Rushie River	Blackie	1938
Fairies of the Trees	Blackie	1940
When Spring Came In at the Window	Blackie	1942
A Child's Garden of Verses (R L Stevenson)	Blackie	1944
Flower Fairies of the Garden	Blackie	1944
Groundsel and Necklaces	Blackie	1946
Flower Fairies of the Wayside	Blackie	1948
Fairies of the Flowers and Trees	Blackie	1950
The Flower Fairy Picture Book	Blackie	1955

Lively Stories	Macmillan	1954
Lively Numbers	Macmillan	1957
Lively Words	Macmillan	1961
Flower Fairies of the Winter	Blackie	1985
Simon the Swan	Blackie	1988

BOOK COVERS

A New Epiphany	SPCK	1919
43 Annuals	Blackie	1920s, 1930s

RELIGIOUS WORKS

'St Cecily's Garden'	1920
Cradle roll design for St Edmund's, Pitlake	1922
Banner design for St Mary's, Sanderstead	1923
Reredos triptych, 'The Feeding of the Five Thousand', for the chapel at Penarth	1929
Triptych, 'The Parable of the Great Supper', for the chapel at St George's, Waddon	1935
'The Seven Sacraments', for the font at St Andrew's, Croydon	1941
Central panel of children's banner, 'St John the Baptist', for Abesford church	1943
Lettering, sword and shield for the mount of the list of men and women serving in the Forces, for St Andrew's, Croydon	1944
Baptismal rolls for St Andrew's, Croydon	1948, 1962
'Out of Great Tribulation', for memorial chapel of Norbury Methodist church	1948
Stained glass window design, 'I am among you as he that serveth' for St Edmund's, Pitlake	1962

AUTHOR'S ACKNOWLEDGEMENTS

I would like to thank Martin West, for introducing me to Cicely Mary Barker; Rosemary Lanning for her original research work; Martin and Hilary Barker, and Geoffrey and Angela Oswald for trusting me with so much reference material and for their friendliness and hospitality; Father Hendry, Father Canon Ingram Hill, Katherine Fairweather, Rosie Wortman, Brenda Litchfield, Mike Miller of Blackie, Michael Heseltine of Sotheby's and Sally Macdonald of Croydon Central Library, for their helpful insights and information; Patricia Wright for her art consultancy; and Debra Clapson for her keying in and her patience.

JANE LAING

ILLUSTRATION ACKNOWLEDGEMENTS

The publishers would like to thank the following for their kind permission to reproduce the photographs and illustrations in this book which appear on the pages listed below:
Martin Barker, 7, 8, 9, 10, 11, 12, 13, 14, 15, 16, 17, 18, 21, 22, 23, 24, 25, 26, 27, 28, 29, 30, 51 (above), 53 (below and right), 57 (below), 61 (below), 63 (above), 70, 72, 73, 76 (below), 79 (below), 101 (below), 103 (above), 109 (below), 115, 119 (above); Sheila Glyn-Jones for material used in her biography of Cicely Mary Barker, *Cicely Mary Barker: A Croydon Artist* published by Croydon Natural History and Scientific Society, 116-17, 118-19, 120, 121, 122: Manchester City Art Galleries, 36; the Medici Society Ltd, 31, 34, 39 (above); National Galleries of Scotland, 33; Geoffrey Oswald, 98.

INDEX

Page numbers in *italics* refer to illustrations.